BMX
Champ

Phil Kettle
illustrated by Craig Smith

Black Hills

Distributed in
the United States of America
by Pacific Learning
P.O. Box 2723
Huntington Beach, CA
92647-0723

Website:
www.pacificlearning.com

Published by Black Hills
(an imprint of Toocool Rules
Pty Ltd)
PO Box 2073
Fitzroy MDC VIC 3065
Australia
61+3+9419-9406

First published in the United States by Black Hills in 2004.
American editorial by Pacific Learning in 2004.
Text copyright © Phillip Kettle, 2001.
Illustration copyright © Toocool Rules Pty Limited, 2001.

 a black dog and Springhill book

Printed in China through Colorcraft Ltd, Hong Kong

ISBN 1 920924 02 7
PL-6201

10 9 8 7 6 5 4 3 2 1   08 07 06 05 04

Contents

Tony

Dog

Toocool

Chapter 1
Top Speed

I could no longer hear the roar of the crowd. The pounding of my heart drowned it out. I was actually at the starting line of the United States BMX Championship.

Tony was beside me.
We had both won pole position.
The flag went down. The race
was on!

I pulled out in front of
Tony and leaned into the first
corner. The curve around the
front porch was tight—the back
wheel spun out. Luckily, I was
able to keep control.

I dropped into a lower gear
and accelerated up the straight.
I was headed for the sweeping
bend that led around the house.
I was almost at top speed by
the time I got there. The crowd
was a blur as I sped past.

3

Tony was still close behind
me and riding fast. I needed to
put some distance between us.
I leaned the bike into the
corner. I was at top speed. Oh
no—my bike began to shimmy
because of its blinding pace.

4

The back wheel started to slide out. I held on tight.
It took all my skill just to keep the bike up. Then, suddenly the front wheel twisted. I went over the handlebars.

The flight through the air didn't hurt at all. It was only when I landed that the pain set in.

Chapter 2
First Aid

Mom ran onto the track. "Toocool! Are you all right? You have to be more careful!"

She didn't know that champions took risks.

I limped off to the side. Tony waved the yellow flag. The race had to be stopped until the wreckage had been cleared.

Mom took me to the first aid station. I got bandages on both knees and both elbows. I wiped a tear from my eye. There must have been some dust in the air.

Then I put on extra safety gear—this made Mom happy.

My bike needed some urgent repairs. Some of my special speed enhancements were damaged.

With great mechanical skill, I taped my racing machine back together. Toocool and his bike were back in business.

The chickens had jumped the course fence and were pecking at the racetrack. When they heard me re-enter the race they flapped back into the stands.

Dog was lying on the grass in the sun. He couldn't handle the race-day tension either. He dove under the house.
I wondered how he was going to see the race from there.

The flag went down. The race was under way again—but something was wrong. My bike was not going as fast as before. The gears felt stiff, and Tony was way ahead of me.

I needed to get going. Toocool felt the need for speed.

Chapter 3
Back on Track

I threw the bike into the first corner. My confidence was building and so was my speed. I flew around the second corner. I sped past the doghouse. I zoomed around the shed. I put my head down and pedaled harder. I was almost at the chicken coop.

Bert the Rooster was at his water dish. He looked up and saw me coming. I saw the panic in his eyes. He took a flying leap across the racetrack. Bert—like everyone else at my house—is an amazing athlete. He cleared the track with feet to spare.

It was time for a pit stop. I dropped the bike and ran toward the snack bar.

"Wipe your feet before you come in," said Mom, "and hang up your helmets."

While we drank our orange
juice, I came up with a plan.

"I think we should make
some changes to the track,"
I whispered. "This track is way
too easy."

Tony agreed.

Chapter 4
In the Tree

We got a big slab of wood from the shed. Then we found a brick. Together, they made an excellent ramp.

The race started again. Our speed built up as we zoomed up the straight together.
I could see the ramp ahead.
I had to be first!

I pedaled faster. Tony moved
out of my way. I waved to him
as I flew past. I hit the ramp at
top speed. It was only then
that I thought about what I
was doing.

Up the ramp my bike went.
I felt as if I had been launched
into space! I knew what it was
like to be a bird.

I looked toward the house.
Mom was looking out the
window with her mouth open.
I looked to the front again.
Oh no! Not the lemon tree!

There was no way I could stop in time—I was riding a powerful machine. Sometimes it had a mind of its own.

I shut my eyes and held on. I did a huge skid and clipped the lemon tree. I hit the ground. Thump!

I lay still. I wasn't sure if I could move. Then I wiggled my toes. They moved. So did my fingers, and my legs, and my arms.

Toocool had survived his death-defying leap!

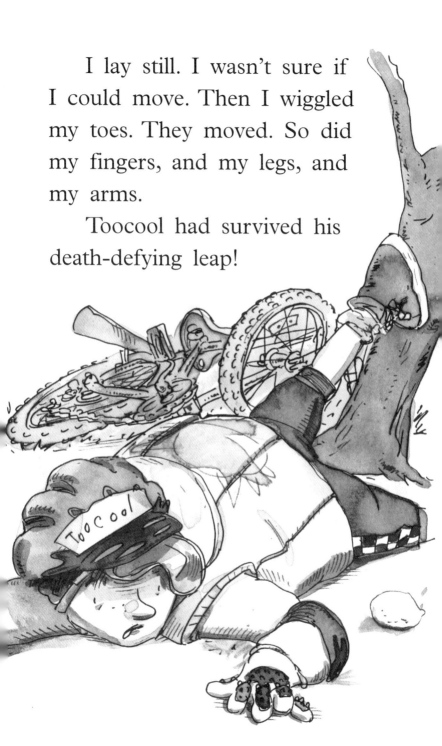

"Toocool! If you ever do that again you're grounded from bike riding for good!" Mom yelled.

I didn't have time to listen. The race was getting too close. Tony had gained on me while I was in the lemon tree.

Chapter 5
Trophy Time

I jumped back on the bike.
I was picking up speed. My
bike chain was making a strange
creaking noise, but the bike still
worked. I slid in and out of the
corners. I had full control now.
I was riding like the true
champion that I was.

It was the last lap and
I was only a few feet behind
Tony. By the time I came
around the second-to-last
corner, I was at top speed.

I cut in front of Tony. He yelled something at me about a blowout, but I kept going. I accelerated up the straight toward the checkered flag.

"Go, Toocool!" I screamed.

I looked behind me. Tony was sprawled across the track. He must have fallen off.

It didn't matter—I was the winner!

I threw my helmet in the air. I waved to the crowd. I was the top BMX rider in the United States! I was winning so many trophies, I would have to get another shelf to display them all.

When the festivities died
down, we dragged Tony's bike
into the pits. I stuck some
patches on the punctures. Tony
went to the first aid station
and Mom stuck some patches
on him.

I could hear the radio in the first aid station. The announcers were talking about surfing. Everyone was talking about the world-class surfers who were coming in to compete.

I hung up my bike helmet. It was time to dig out my surfboard.

The End!

Toocool's
Bike Glossary

Accelerated—Toocool accelerated. That means he went faster.

Blowout—A tire that is instantly flat or destroyed because of a puncture or other damage.

BMX—This is short for "Bicycle Motocross." It is an exciting sport that has races, and freestyle competitions that test rider skill and bravery.

The pits—The place where you get repairs done during the race.

Puncture—A hole in your tire is called a puncture.

Toocool's Backyard
Bike Track

The Garage

Dog's Place

Toolshed

Lemon Tree

The U
Champion
BMX Tra

Start and
Finish

Chickens

The Straight

Toocool's Bedroom

First Aid Area

Toocool's Quick Summary
Bike Racing

The first bike wasn't that fast. It had no pedals! It had to be pushed along by the rider's feet. After that, other bikes were invented. They had pedals, but they were uncomfortable. People called them "bone shakers."

Now bikes are cool. They can be used for transportation, and for fun, and for sports. I use my bike for all these things.

The most famous road race is called the Tour de France. I plan to ride in it soon. It's in France, so I'll have to save up for the airplane ticket.

Mountain bike racing is also fun. You need a bike with a really strong frame. You have to ride up and down trails. You also have to wear a full-face helmet. It's really hard work.

My favorite kind of bike riding is BMX racing. BMX tracks can be really rough. They have steep banks and lots of bumps. There's speed and dirt. If you're really lucky there's mud—which is fantastic!

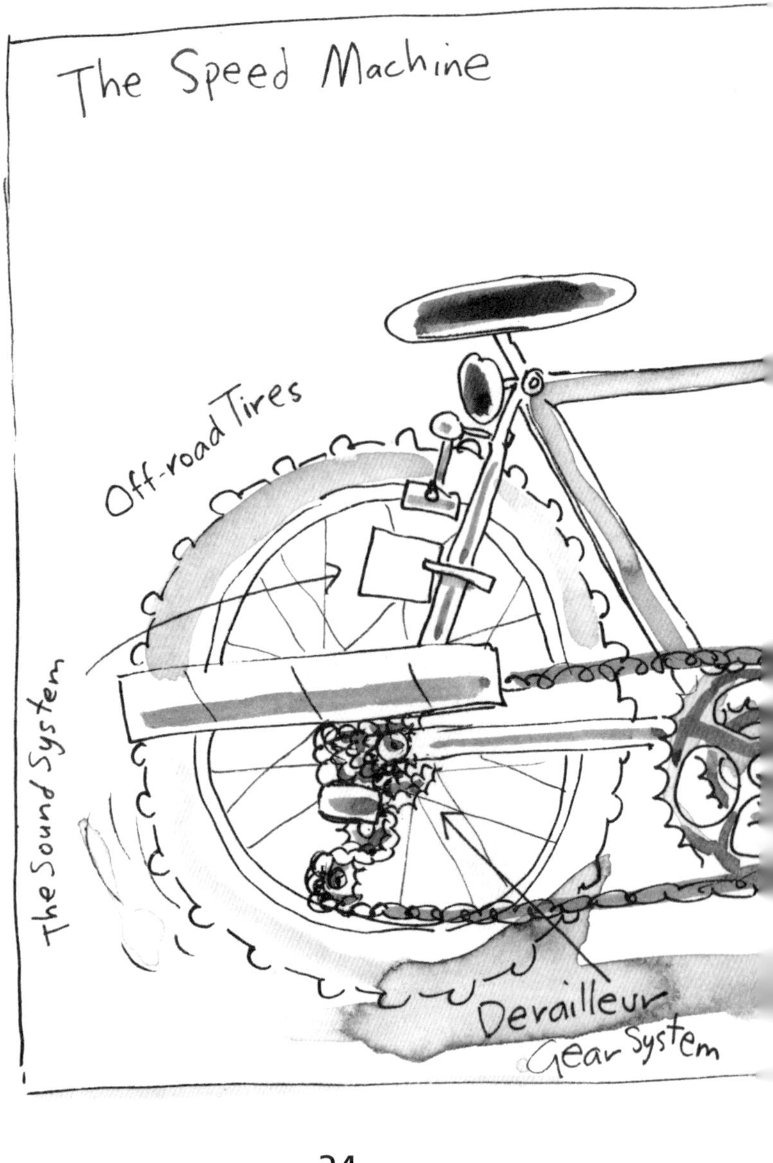

The **Bike**

The Speed Machine

Off-road Tires

The Sound System

Derailleur Gear System

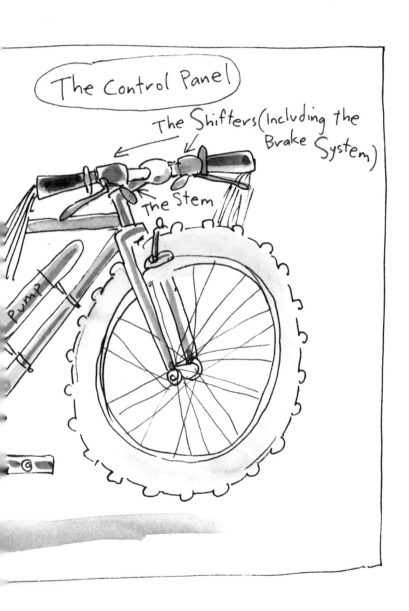

The Control Panel

The Shifters (Including the Brake System)

The Stem

Pump

Q & A with **Toocool**
He Answers His Own Questions

What kind of bike do you have?

My bike is a BMX-ready machine, but I can modify it if I want to. That way I can go in any kind of bike race. For the Tour de France, I'll turn it into a road bike. It will be the fastest racing bike ever.

How many times have you fallen off your bike?

Champions never fall off, but sometimes there are problems (like lemon trees). Or there might be a dog on the track. When that happens, even champions have crashes. I've had a few crashes, but I've never just fallen off.

Does it hurt when you crash?

Not really. I always wear a helmet. If it's a big race, I wear all the other safety gear, such as kneepads and gloves. I'm more worried about my bike. I don't want it to get scratched or bent. I don't have a fast pit crew. It takes them forever just to change a tire, so I try not to hurt the bike.

Do you enter many races?

Yes. I enter lots of races. I enter road races and mountain bike races and BMX races. I win them all. Dog thinks he can beat me, but he can't. He barks too much, and he keeps trying to bite my wheels.

What's the best thing about being a champion bike rider?

It's being able to ride faster than the wind. I like having my picture in the paper, and giving TV interviews. I also like riding home from school fast, so I can get something to eat.

Where do you keep your bike?

I'm supposed to keep my bike in the toolshed, but sometimes I forget. The other day, I left it in the backyard. It was outside all night and it rained. The next morning, my bike was all wet, and my helmet was full of water. I hope I don't get a rusty chain.

Did you ever have training wheels?

Never. I never, ever had training wheels. I just climbed on, and off I went. I'm a natural.

Bike Quiz
How Much Do You Know about Bikes?

Q1 What do you do when you come to a stop sign?
A. Stop pedaling. *B.* Stop and look both ways before going on.
C. Go home.

Q2 What side of the road should you ride on?
A. The left-hand side. *B.* The right-hand side. *C.* The middle.

Q3 Are you allowed to ride on the sidewalk?
A. Never. *B.* Only when the road signs tell you that it's okay.
C. All the time.

Q4 The Tour de France is held in which country?
A. USA. *B.* China. *C.* France.

Q5 How many wheels does a tricycle have?
A. Five. *B.* Four. *C.* Three.

Q6 Is bike riding an Olympic sport?
A. Always. *B.* Sometimes. *C.* Never.

Q7 How many wheels does a unicycle have?
A. Four. *B.* None. *C.* One.

Q8 Should you wear a helmet when you ride your bike?
A. Always. *B.* Sometimes. *C.* Only if it's raining.

Q9 What would you do if you got a blowout?

A. Get Mom to fix it. **B.** Get Dad to fix it. **C.** Fix it yourself.

Q10 What would you do if you came in second against Toocool?

A. Try harder next time. **B.** Cry and go home. **C.** Be very happy that you came in second against the champion.

ANSWERS

1 B.   *2* B.   *3* B.

4 C.   *5* C.   *6* A.

7 C.   *8* A.   *9* C.

10 C.

If you got ten questions right, you can join the Tour de France. If you got more than five right, you shouldn't go past your driveway. If you got fewer than five right, you should stay away from anything with wheels.

TOOCOOL

Surfing Pro

It's summer vacation and there's a surfing contest to win. **Toocool** waxes down his twin fin and hits the waves.

Titles in the Toocool series